RUBANK BOOK OF CLARINET SOLOS
EASY LEVEL

PLAYBACK+
Speed · Pitch · Balance · Loop

CONTENTS

To access recordings and PDF accompaniments visit:
www.halleonard.com/mylibrary

5891-7797-7012-9325

ISBN 978-1-4950-6504-0

RUBANK®

HAL•LEONARD® CORPORATION
7777 W. BLUEMOUND RD. P.O. BOX 13819 MILWAUKEE, WI 53213

Visit Hal Leonard Online at
www.halleonard.com

Ode To Music

Op. 10, No. 3

Clarinet

F. Chopin
Arranged by Art Jolliff

Andante

From "Pathetique Symphony", Op. 74

Clarinet

Peter Ilyich Tchaikovsky
Arranged by Henry W. Davis

Jolly Coppersmith

Clarinet

C. Peters
Arranged by Art Joliff

Cielito Lindo
(Beautiful Heaven)

Clarinet

C. Fernandez
Arranged by Art Jolliff

Largo
From "New World Symphony"

Clarinet

Anton Dvorak
Arranged by Henry W. Davis

The Lonely Birch Tree

Russian Folk Song

Clarinet

Arranged by
Clarence E. Hurrell

Melody
Op. 68, No. 1

Clarinet

Robert Schumann
Arranged by Henry W. Davis

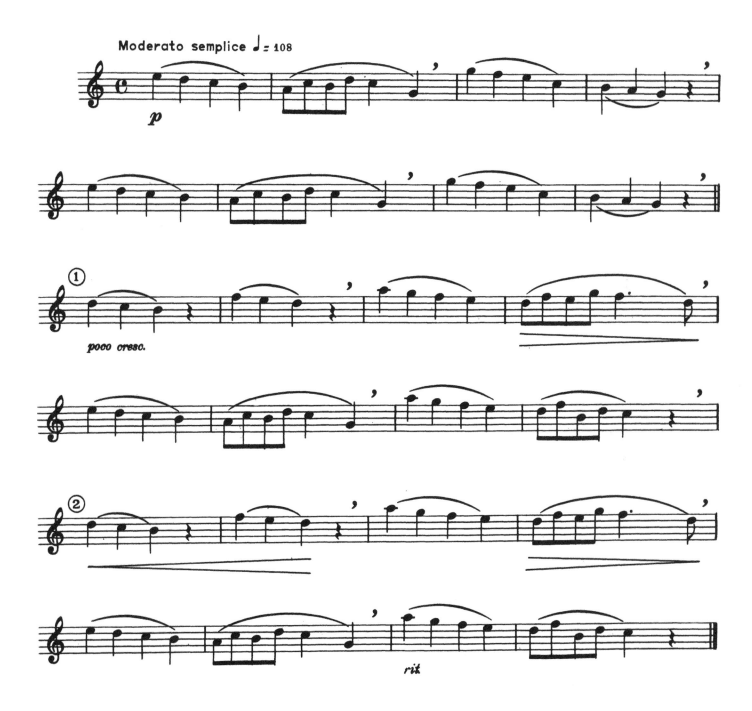

March Of A Marionette

Clarinet

Chas. Gounod
Arranged by Harold L. Walters

Allegretto (♩. = 96)

Piano

(8)

mp

f

(16)

mp

(24)

f p f p

f

(32)

mp

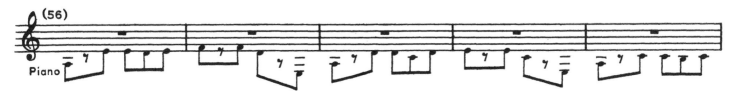

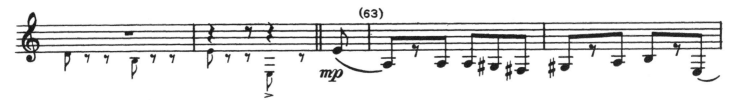

Sleeping Beauty

Waltz Theme From The Ballet

Clarinet

Peter Ilyich Tschaikowsky
Arranged by Henry W. Davis

Spirit Dance

From The Opera "Orpheus"

Clarinet

C. W. von Gluck
Arranged by Henry W. Davis

Unfinished Symphony
Themes From The First Movement

Clarinet

Franz Schubert
Arranged by Henry W. Davis